#FILLYOURTANK

Be authentically YOU!

From the Author:

In the quest to find what really filled my tank, it has
taken a lot of prayer to understand my true strength and
embrace the uncomfortable. Afterall, if you don't sit in the
uncomfortable you'll never know how to evolve from your
core. I believe we are all here on this planet for a reason.
I believe we all have the opportunity to grow and live
the life we want by doing what fills our tanks.

You cannot throw all of your pain up against the wall,
hope it sticks and the universe magically saves you
from hurt. You have to do the hard work. You have
to show up for yourself first. That means getting real,
raw and owning your shit as is. The journey is well worth it.

Xo - LH

This book is dedicated to my daughter:

My beautiful daughter, Kelis. May you always know your
worth and continue to strive for all the things in life
that make your soul sing. You are wise beyond your years.
Smart, witty, insanely funny and beautiful. Remember,
beauty starts from within and radiates out.

You come from a long line of women with deep strength,
character and wisdom. Never settle for less than and always
rise to the challenge. You may hear a million no's and
experience failures, but remember they do not define you.
Keep going!

You are a light for so many and your heart is as big as
the ocean, but remember you can't carry the world on
your shoulders. Find balance, set healthy boundaries
and never stop praying. Relish in the small things
and remember to smile even on the bad days.

Do all things with love and dance. A lot.
Love, Mom

Instead of running away
from what scares you,
go towards it.
Follow your heart,
There is always magic
in following your bliss.

No great love has ever come from something rushed.

Go at the pace that works for you and only you.
That is where true love begins.

*Make time
for the people
who truly matter
in your life.*

Not the ones who you think are channels to you getting ahead.

Far too often do we cancel, reschedule or just not respond
to the people in our lives who are important. We all have
been guilty of this; making some people in our lives
a priority who seem to add value in the moment over
the ones who are there consistently and genuinely.
Consistency should run parallel on all levels of your
friendships and relationships.

Let's not wait for tragedy to strike to reflect on the
"I should have or I wish I had done xyz" before you really
make people in your life who truly matter a priority.

THERE
IS VALUE
IN THE
STRUGGLE

In everything, there is a lesson. In everything, there is value. No matter how big or small the struggle is, there is value in learning and growing from any situation.

Struggle does not have to equal bad. There is a lot of good that comes out of the struggle. It just depends what set of lenses you choose to view from.

Be
unfiltered
truth

There is power in truth. Positive power in being, telling, and living truth. Be that. The kind of truth you seek.

Marinate in moments of joy

Lean into your happy. Be curious about it. Absorb it.
It's good for the soul.

**Going forward
requires you to launch.
You cannot launch
if you don't step forward.**

To do the things that are scariest or exciting requires an act
of action and launching full speed ahead with both feet in.

You will not have all the answers to what's next,
but embrace it with courage and vulnerability.

stand armored in your *passion*

Listen to the voice within that roars with excitement when it thinks about your passion; when it feels like sun glistening off the lake or taste like the first sip of coffee on an easy Sunday morning.

Stand blissfully armored in your passion. Only you can make it what it is. After all, it's your dream.

Transparency
and truth with oneself is key to transformation of any kind.

Transparency can bring out the biggest of "aha" moments within ourselves. It is in those moments you begin to experience the beauty of where you stand and what you stand for. Go in the direction of transparency led with authenticity.

SOMETIMES YOU HAVE TO
change the players
IN ORDER TO
change the game

give yourself permission to *dream*

Your dreams. Your passion. Your path. Download all
of the possibilities. Let no one tell you otherwise.

Live your truth.
Speak your truth.
Stand present in your own power.

There is no time like the present to show up
fully present in your truth. Be who you are.

Be compassionate with your soul and give yourself
the type of love you daydream about having with another.

Love all of you. Through and through.

BE STRATEGIC.
HUMBLE YOURSELF
AND EXECUTE.

Strategy, humbleness and execution. Without those key
ingredients, ideas are just ideas, relationships and connections
are just as-is and goals are likely to be stuck in progress.

Give yourself a pass or two but remain
focused on the bigger vision. You are capable!

The process of change is not always appealing, but it is always necessary.

Change creates visibility into things you might have turned a blind eye to because it was better to stay in routine. It was comfortable. It was easy. Embrace the journey of change. It will always create moments of clarity and opportunities to reflect on what is, what was and what's ahead.

Colorful vs. Sincere

Colorful, often times, is covered up to appear like vibrant spring flowers when it's truly a hefty load of BS. Sincerity, when it's done right, is authentically planted in deep roots. Showing up as-is. Flaws and all. It shows up without judgement, it knows we are all a work in progress and no one is better or less than the next. It's not a popularity contest. It's inclusive and grounded.

We have all played one of these parts or both. Something to remember: You cannot play in both sections and be genuine. Know yourself enough to be better than showing up as colorful bullshit.

GOALS. PASSION. DREAMS.

_____

Wrap your heart around each one.

Be your biggest fan and loudest cheerleader even when
it feels daunting and uncertain. Your goals, passion
and dreams are celebrated in your heart.

Live your happy out loud.

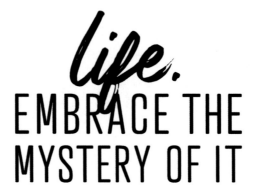

EMBRACE THE MYSTERY OF IT

Love the mystery. Once you stop fearing and start indulging in life, there is something it teaches us all; to let go. Worrying about what could, should or would only blocks your ability to fully absorb this planet you were blessed to wake up on today. Once again, get out of your own fuckin' way and live life.

Be spontaneous. Be loving. Be fuckin' courageous.

There comes a time in life when you don't give a damn what other people think of you.
LIVE. YOUR. LIFE.

Be bold in the pursuit of your own self-acceptance.
Too often we are plagued with what a person or
groups think of us. Don't desire to fit in.

The people who are meant to be there will be.
And, let the ship sail for the ones who are not.

Let it go and live YOUR life! Life is too short and precious
to spend on folks that don't matter in the end.

Create the landscape you want to live.

Show up for yourself first to fully capture the essence
of YOUR own internal beauty. Some might say "easier
said than done" or nix this entire process. You do yourself
a disservice in just talking about how you want life to
change or your circumstances to change.

Wanting to feel different or better while existing
in this life requires action. You cannot find a slice
of calming or self-approval if you do not address
the issues or the ache that exist in your everyday.

You deserve the right to show up for yourself
and live the life that makes you smile and glow
at all the good even during the challenges.

GET OUT OF YOUR OWN WAY

There may be a million things you think are standing
in the way of your dreams. Perhaps it's just you. Get out
of your own way and go in the direction of your dreams.
Our dreams are certainly bigger than our fears.
To do the work you love from an authentic place
with positive intention is the only approval you need.
It is the only success that matters.

Pay attention to the little things because, sometimes, the big details are in the little things.

Let that sink in... Grand gestures are not always necessary. Sometimes it's as simple as listening, being self-aware and showing people compassion.

Good, kind, authentic human connection.
Share in the small gestures. Genuine love resides there.

Opportunities come by how you present yourself in the world.

When we are open to receiving certain things in life, a shift happens. Opportunities that may not have shown up previously, do.

Collective agreement with yourself in creating space for growth and opportunity equals a level playing field to move in the direction of your goals and dreams.

TURN
obstacles
INTO
opportunities

Don't sit out on an opportunity because there
are obstacles that show up as uncomfortable
moments or appear unobtainable.

Your biggest win is showing up as the best version
of yourself, regardless of the struggle, and giving
it all you've got. Everything you want is worth trying.
Go for it!

*Never quit on the day
you are ready to quit.*

That might just be the day you give your best
performance, speech or have the courage to do
the thing you have been wanting to do most.

Don't give up!

I AM
YOU ARE
WE ARE

WORTHY

In case you forgot.

A friendly reminder... Ask for what you want. Work towards what you want. Achieve your greater vision. You are worthy of all the things that your heart desires. Align yourself with positive intention and act accordingly. The plan has been there all along. You just have to be open to receiving.

CONFRONT CHANGE

Being complacent is self-torture resulting in doing the hard task of confronting what weighs you down, removing yourself from toxic relationships and friendships, not setting boundaries or running away from opportunities because of self-doubt.

The moment you find strength in your voice, you create a whole new level of change within yourself and your life. Change takes time, but when you make YOU the priority of that change, it's all worth it.

INSPECT WHAT YOU EXPECT

Reevaluate your expectations with clear views. Align your wants, needs and desires in a way that works for you personally and professionally. If in that review process something doesn't work for you, it's okay to take a step back.

You cannot expect something to happen when you have not defined what it is that works for you or does not work for you. Be clear in your boundaries and self-aware of your expectations.

Set
boundaries.

Stand
with your boundaries.

Boundaries impact many areas of our lives. Set healthy boundaries to protect your soul, space, relationships, mindset and lifestyle. You are the leader of the line where your boundaries start and end. Everyone else can fall in line as you stand firm in them.

If you are scared to take chances, you'll never have the answers.

GO FOR IT

Chances are you want to and you talk yourself out of it.
We've all done it. Fear of rejection, fear of moving forward,
fear of asking for what you want and need because
of the strong hold fear presents and the uncertainty
of one's reactions.

It can be paralyzing at times, but pull strength
from a deeper place. It's a game changer.
Take it one step at a time and one day at a time.

Let your positive inner voice be your compass to tackle
any hurdle while fear takes a back seat.

BEING MEAN IS NOT *sexy*

IS IT KIND?

Your words have power and your actions have meaning.
Be aware of both and then some. Move through the world
with kindness in your heart for yourself and others.
Anything other is not a good look.

The most important trip you can take in life is meeting people *halfway*

EFFORT + ACTION

Combined can create space for openness
and understanding. Sometimes it may take tough,
uncomfortable conversations to get to a place of
understanding, connection and unity. There may be days
where it seems effortless and the action is beautifully
executed. You'll think you don't need to do any
self-reflection or work. Wrong. Regardless of how things
flow, having a heart that is open and willing to meet
people halfway, no matter the challenge, will go a
long way. There is always room for improvement
in the space of connection and people.

ELEVATE YOUR GAME

STEP UP

We often sit back and think should have, could have
and would have done xyz if only... Excuses never get anyone
anywhere. You can't expand and improve yourself in areas
of growth personally or professionally if you don't step up.
Sitting idle or settling is tapping on the shoulder of mediocre.
You're better than that.

YOUR ATTITUDE
determines
YOUR ALTITUDE

It's all in your mindset. Positive attitude. Positive actions.
Positive results. Good people. Good energy.
Put that on repeat.

When you feel love, act on it. Speak your heart. Be truthful. Remain open.

Be brave in your loving! Be brave in all the ways you love, from your family, your husband, wife or partner to the wonderful stranger who flashed you the best smile you've seen all day. Give open-hearted love back!!

With love comes compassion that eases and enriches the soul. Do all the feel-good, loving kind of things. It's much more flavorful than the opposite.

choose to take risks on behalf of our own HAPPINESS

CHOOSE

All risks are not bad risks. Stepping out of your comfort zone and into the unknown is often the best blessing you can give yourself.

Choose your happy!

Explore ⬅ Unfold

Give yourself permission to reflect and recharge.
Reflection and recharging allows room to be present.
Slow down. Give life a thank you. After all, you cannot
do today over and tomorrow is not guaranteed.

Remove the mask.

Hiding behind the false version of yourself restricts
you from real authentic connection. The real version
of yourself is the best version.

Whatever you do
or wherever you go,
go with what
feels right.
Enjoy the moment
for as long as you can.

life is not a
rehearsal

Just in case, you forgot. One life. One shot.
Whatever that is, make sure you give it all you got.
Life is full of uncertainty, but it is all in the
uncertainty that we grow.

do not indulge your ego at the expense of your *soul*

Allow your ego to sit on a side that only the most organic and authentic experiences align with your soul. The real you always looks better.

Be authentically intentional.

Empathetic, compassionate and inclusive.
Be that. Rise up!

SHIFT YOUR FOCUS

If you do not stand for something, you will fall for anything. Stand for what matters most to you. Stand in solidarity for those you believe in fighting for. Stand firm in your ability to have your own voice.

DO NOT SETTLE FOR
stagnant
OR
mediocre

Break down barriers. For every million no's all you need
is one yes. That yes matters. Run with it. Relish in it
and make beautiful magic out of it. Your goals
and dreams have no limits.

action
is more than just
a six-letter word

_____

Make sure your action is aligned with follow-through.

do not
change
to fit in

If people cannot love and accept you for you, it is time to find new people to surround yourself with and indulge in loving yourself more.

PERSISTENCE PASSION PERSEVERANCE

Persistence, passion and perseverance, when equipped with patience, creates better perspective and growth.

Stop looking for attention from others and start focusing on yourself.
Be your own driving force of acceptance.

There you go again... Hoping someone accepts you, praises your accomplishments and admires any and all things you. And when they don't, there is this self-doubt, playing the victim syndrome and questioning the validation of who you are in a ridiculous state of not being self-aware.

STOP that!

Start accepting yourself first, praising your own accomplishments and checking your faults while living in reality. Once you do this, you realize how to filter the background noise of judgement accordingly.

DO NOT HIT THE SNOOZE BUTTON ON LIFE.

dare to be different

Stand in your own power!

You just might be surprised by the glorious outcome.

wonder with
a curious heart

_____

Have intention that dances like a flame.
That is where genuine connection is made.

GET YOUR EGO IN CHECK

LOOK WITHIN

You may go through a breakdown before a breakthrough.
The only way this can happen is when you stop
and check your ego. We are often so self-absorbed
with a life that looks like everything is alright to those
on the outside that you forget what REAL really
looks like. Imposters walk among us daily. We know them,
we work with them, some are our friends and family.
We often seek them out for advice because we think
we see something else.

False appearances appearing real. Open your eyes
and your soul. A self-check and look within to reset your
ego is always a better look than being an imposter.

you cannot defend what you do not know

Do not assume. Seek first to understand. Equip yourself with the tools and knowledge to understand everything before you act on anything.

recalibrate

Know when you need to take a step back,
realign and reconstruct your day to day.
Take charge!

Life is too short to sit with a toxic heart.

The things you harbor or hold resentment about
are really holding you hostage from moving forward
in your life. Work towards healing in whatever
capacity you can. It is healthy and good for your soul.

the heart is a

wonderful place

you can tuck
people or things in

Don't let your heart be hardened by the past,
the broken or the unexplainable. Be open to
allowing your heart to receive all things good.

TAKE YOUR
PAST
AND FIND
YOUR
PATH

You gain traction, clarity and growth by allowing experiences to propel you forward. Launch into a new phase of your life with appreciation for learning from the past. Each step is progress.

sometimes the *unfamiliar route* is the right road to be on

The unknown is often life's gift of teachable
moments. Every road leads somewhere
and there is purpose on every path.

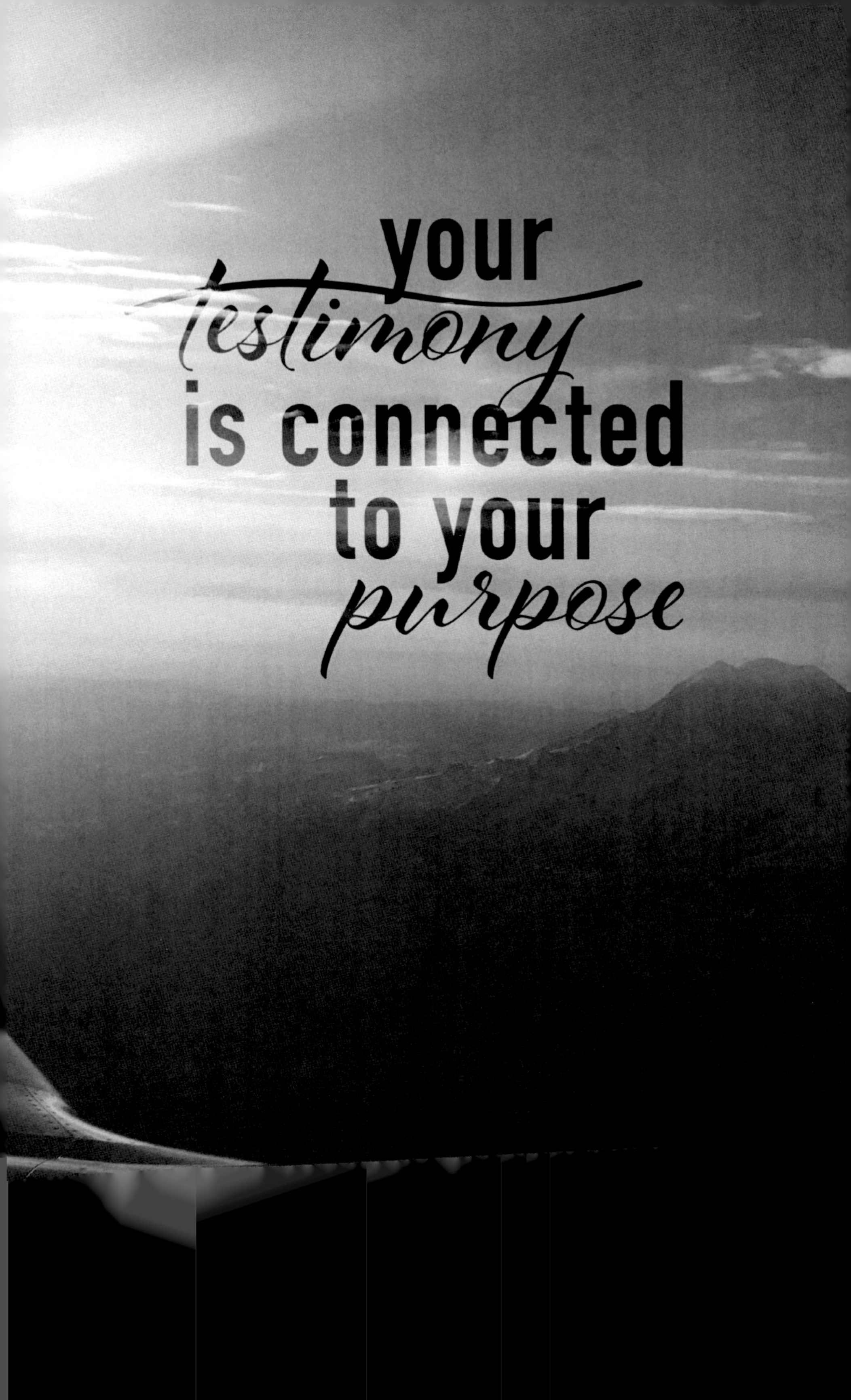
your testimony is connected to your purpose

DO NOT ALLOW
SOMEONE ELSE
TO DEFINE
you

Remember when... You allowed fear to settle in
comfortably and dictate every aspect of your life?
When you allowed years, days and months to go by
realizing you haven't lived for yourself?

Remember your happiness cannot be defined by
someone else. Happiness starts within yourself.
Don't allow someone to say "you don't make me happy"
and own their chunk of bullshit. First, we have to make
ourselves happy in order to be happily productive,
effective and on a path of growth with anything or anyone.

Do you first. The rest will fall into place;
the right people and the right opportunities.

Accept
no one else's
definition of *your life*

Your journey is your journey. Your life is your life.
Your mess is your mess. No one knows the
functions of all those things better than you do.
Regardless if it falls into the messy category at times.

Embrace who you are.

Define your life by living YOUR life.

Success on the outside depends on our ability to execute inside.

Love yourself, nurture your soul and expand your belief in you.

be the
ARCHITECT
of your
LIFE

Plan. Design. Start construction. With dedication
and passion in your corner, you can build
and create the life you want. Take time to know
what it is you really want and work from there.
Anything is possible.

BE BRAVE
IN ALL THE WAYS
YOU LOVE

Love can be magical, unruly, beautiful and sometimes
messy. No matter what series of events you
encounter, at the center of it all, let love always
be your hearts compass. Be brave in love.

Some people may not fit your life's recipe.

Some will stay and some will go. You can learn from every encounter and do your best to get clear on what and who is best suited in your world. Have no regrets when it comes to making sure those in your life are aligned with you and operate from a positive place.

Let that shit go!

Stop trying to control situations, or find fault
in people or things. Life is too short to be
held captive by resentment.

FOLLOW YOUR
passion

Following your passion is about finding
your voice. Once you have found it, you have
the divine responsibility to use it.

TAKE
accountability

When you begin to accept your flaws and take
ownership for the role you play in life, you understand
that integrity and authenticity will be the best
version you can show up as.

No matter how steep, rocky or hard it feels to get there, *challenge yourself* to continue moving forward.
Coming back down, or completing the task at hand is icing on the cake.
You gain clarity in the beautiful things you can do when you are focused on your *inner peace*.

it's all in the *experience*

At first contact, you have the ability to make it great and meaningful. Remember the experience you would want and mirror that.

PASSION WITH PURPOSE

Heartfelt, fiery, purposefully, driven passion done on the heels with purpose is the best driving force. Sometimes the silent rewards are the greatest rewards.

You don't need a spotlight shining on what you do at all times and it doesn't always require a social media post or a collage of "look at what I've done." Let your work speak for itself, but please remember to keep the purpose positively intentional. There is a greater vision for us all and how we execute says it all.

Clarity is magnetic.

Clarity creates perspective. The space given
to create this inward and outward is a
magical transformation.

LIVE LIFE TO THE
fullest

Try not to have regrets.
Soak it up, be your own pilot and soar.

CHALLENGE YOURSELF TO:

_____

Listen more. Be vulnerable and approach
things with an open mind. Open heart. Open mind.

The shift begins with you.

Stop seeking life among things that cannot give you life.

Life is not about forcing things to be. Allow organic
connections and authentic layers of people in.
And, love yourself enough to know:
self-love gives you life.

if you want to fly,
give up
the things that
weigh you down

Let go of dead weight. Rise above and fly!

Love looks like: Trust, forgiveness, compassion, encouragement and acceptance.

Go there. Be that. Absorb it.

Make them positively powerful!

A hard obstacle
does not define you.
How you handle it does.
Align your mind, body
and soul with perseverance.

consistency, tenacity and follow-through

They are led by passion that helps build and achieve goals.

TAKE CARE OF YOU!

You have to secure your own mask before you
can secure others. Know what you need to move
through the debris of life before taking
on everyone else's problems.

challenge yourself
to do the
unimaginable

Sitting idle equals stale. Sitting inspired
and fueled equals a magical breakthrough.

feedback is information, not definition.

Be open to feedback but not imprisoned by it. The ability to take feedback is important, but what you do with it is even more important. You are never too old to learn.

there is
beauty
in your journey

It may seem messy and at times relentlessly tiring.
Trust the process. Breathe a light of acceptance
and embrace the beautiful mess or glorious
moments of sunshine in your journey.

enjoy
what was
and
what will be

There is magic in middle.

Let your faith be bigger than your fears.

Your dreams will be challenged. Your patience will be tested. Your goals will feel hard to accomplish.

Be careful how you judge.

Do not sleep on the ones who struggle, because their struggle could end up being their greatest weapon. A quiet fire that will propel them past your doubts.

Lift them up, be a leader and show support. We are all in this together.

A title does not make you *a good leader*

Empathy, listening, trust and the need to see one
succeed are a few good characteristics of a good leader.

Do not be blinded or bullied into thinking someone
can treat you other than the above because of their title.

You create
opportunities
by asking for them.

POSITIVE THOUGHTS
produce
POSITIVE ACTIONS

When you have positive intention, you automatically
schedule your brain in thinking beyond the struggle.
You'll see light at the end of the tunnel
in minutes, hours and days ahead.

absorb your blessings, not your blockings

Relish in the grateful zone. Too often we sit in a place of feeling sorry for ourselves. Not everything will go as planned or as easy as you want it to be. What is important are the blessings that do come your way. Big or small. Absorb them. Learn to lean into them and understand there is more where that came from. Be grateful and trust the process.

commitment
&
flexibility

Stay committed to your decisions and dreams.
Stay flexible in your approach.

when you tone things down, you drown out your

voice

Fuck everything that tries to silence you!

you are more
POWERFUL
than you know

Show them what you are made of. Challenge them
to see the version they thought you were
as a blurry vision in their rearview.

You are not your failures.

You are not your depression or anxiety.
YOUR strength is greater than the obstacles
that try to stand in your way. Believe in the
positive power and strength that resides within.

TRUST YOUR GUT.

It's your inner compass. There is a voice that whispers
from deep within. Trust that. If it doesn't feel right,
it's probably not right. If it feels good and like you
should take a leap of faith, go for it. Listen to your
own voice not the voices of many that tend to drown
out your own. Your gut will guide you. It always does.
You just have to be open and aware of what self
direction looks and feels like.

THE TRUTH.
It is always refreshing.

Honest and real. There is no better way to show
up for yourself and those around you.
The truth is friendly.

Show up for your life.

DON'T SIT OUT

Some days feel like Groundhog Day, I know.
Just remember you woke up today! That in itself
is reason to show up for yourself.

Ignite your inner spark!

Relish in the possibilities.
Dream. Set goals. Execute.

GREATER *transformation* TAKES PLACE *internally*

Acknowledgements

Without passion and dedication, #FillYourTank could not
have become what it is today. The support and collaboration
in designing this book has truly brought it to life. More than
I had imagined. I am immensely grateful for my tribe,
who have pushed me to continue doing this work and have
reminded me the world needs more of this. On a quest
to continue filling our tanks, we are here to ride the
wave in this crazy, beautiful world. Living our truth from
all aspects of authenticity.

Be truth. Be authentic. Be YOU.

Book design by Jinger Hendricks
Author headshot by Robert Jones
Photography by LaEisha Howard

ISBN: 978-0-692-82414-6 (paperback)

Made in the USA
Monee, IL
10 April 2021